Kiss Me, You Fool

I'm in the Mood for Love

Andrew Vines

 Clarkson N. Potter, Inc./Publishers New York
DISTRIBUTED BY CROWN PUBLISHERS, INC.

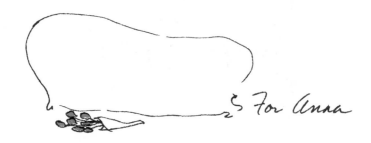

Published by Clarkson N. Potter, Inc., One Park Avenue,
New York, New York 10016 and simultaneously in Canada by
General Publishing Company Limited.
Manufactured in the United States of America

Library of Congress Cataloging in Publication Data
Vines, Andrew.
Kiss me, you fool.
1. Dating (Social customs)—Caricatures and cartoons.
2. Love—Caricatures and cartoons. 3. American wit and
humor, pictorial. I. Title.
NC1429.V58A4 1984   741.5'973   84-18106
ISBN 0-517-55470-4
10 9 8 7 6 5 4 3 2 1
First Edition

Contents

Finding a Date

HAVEN'T I SEEN YOU
SOMEPLACE BEFORE?

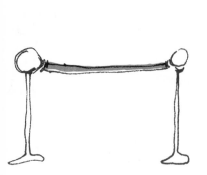

DID ANY OF YOU GUYS HAPPEN TO CATCH THE ARTICLE IN THE <u>NEW ENGLAND</u> <u>JOURNAL</u> <u>OF</u> <u>MEDICINE</u> ABOUT HOT TUBS AND THE TRANSMITTAL OF COMMUNICABLE DISEASES?

LINDA, WHEN ARE YOU GOING TO REALIZE THAT THERE'S NO SUCH THING AS A PURELY PLATONIC RELATIONSHIP?

BY THE WAY, JUDY,
I LOVE YOUR HAIR.

SORRY, FRED, BUT JOYCE
AND I DON'T DANCE.
WE JUST ROAM.

The worst pickup lines

The smoothest pickup line

EXCUSE ME, BUT COULD YOU PLEASE PASS THE KETCHUP,

A KNIFE, YOUR PHONE NUMBER, A NAPKIN, AND THE SALT?

The First Date

YES, IT WAS A WONDERFULLY UNUSUAL DATE, BILL. I'VE NEVER BEEN THROUGH A CAR WASH IN A CONVERTIBLE BEFORE.

DO

Flaunt your worldliness

I TAKE A TRIP TO SOME
EXOTIC PLACE EVERY MONTH.
AT LEAST THAT'S HOW I FEEL AFTER
I READ MY LATEST ISSUE OF
NATIONAL GEOGRAPHIC.

Display a unique talent

IF YOU THINK THAT'S GOOD,
YOU SHOULD SEE HER DO IT WITH
THE MEDALLIONS OF VEAL.

DO

Allude to your vast wealth

Empathize

THEN, ANNE, MY THIRD WIFE, TURNED TO ME AND SAID, "I'M TIRED OF YOUR IDIOSYNCRATIC NONSENSE. IF YOU WANT TO JOIN THE CIRCUS, GO AHEAD. BUT I'M STAYING RIGHT HERE IN BAYONNE, WITH OUR BABY."

WHAT A KILLJOY!

DON'T

Ask for favors

Be too revealing

DON'T

Be inattentive

Come on too strong

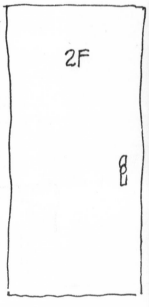

The Blind Date

I'M LOOKING FORWARD TO MEETING
YOU TOO, LOU. LET'S JUST HOPE YOU'RE
NOT A TOTAL DISAPPOINTMENT.

Was he

TOO BORING

TOO INTERESTING

TOO TRENDY

TWO-FACED

TOO INTROVERTED

"...COME THROUGH FOR ME NEW YORK, NEW YORK."

TOO EXTROVERTED

TOO HANDSOME

TOO UGLY

TOO CHEAP

ALL RIGHT, THIS IS THE PLAN.
YOU GO IN AND FIND A TICKET
STUB ON THE FLOOR. THEN BRING IT
OUT TO ME AND I'LL SNEAK IN.

Sex

HEY, I DON'T THINK THIS IS WHAT I MEANT WHEN I ASKED YOU TO SLEEP WITH ME.

WHAT EXACTLY ARE YOU TRYING TO DO WITH YOUR TOE?!
LOUISE, THAT'S NOT MY TOE.

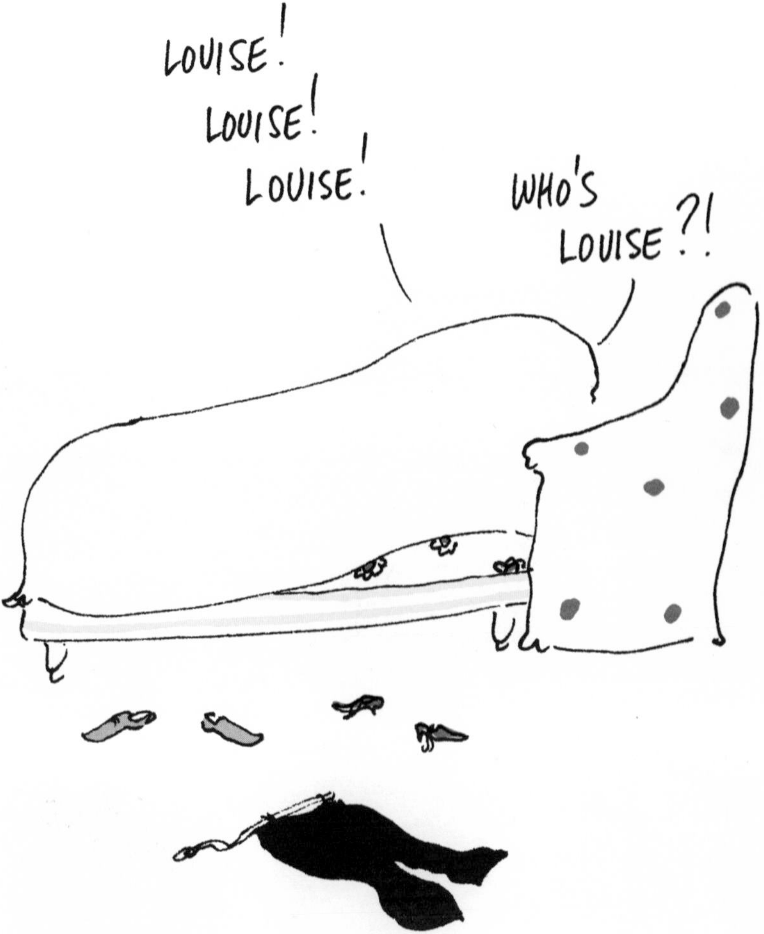
LOUISE!
LOUISE!
LOUISE!
WHO'S LOUISE?!

Taking a Break

RUDOLFO, I REALIZE YOU ARE THE RICHEST MAN IN THE WORLD, AND I DO LOVE YOU, BUT YOU CAN'T EXPECT ME TO ELOPE WITH YOU JUST LIKE THAT.

BETTER SUBLET YOUR APARTMENT FIRST.

GOOD POINT

I REALLY NEED A BREAK FROM THIS DATING SCENE.
ME TOO. AFTER ALL WE DON'T WANT TO END UP LIKE JOYCE.
IS SHE STILL TALKING TO HERSELF?
MM...HMM. ALL SHE SAYS IS "DINNER AND A MOVIE SOUNDS NICE. PICK ME UP AROUND EIGHTISH!"

IT'S ONE TWO CHA-CHA-CHA. WHY DO YOU KEEP ADDING AN EXTRA STEP?!!

NO. I'M SORRY, I REFUSE TO SIT HERE ON A SATURDAY NIGHT AND WATCH "LOVE BOAT."

The worst place to be without a date

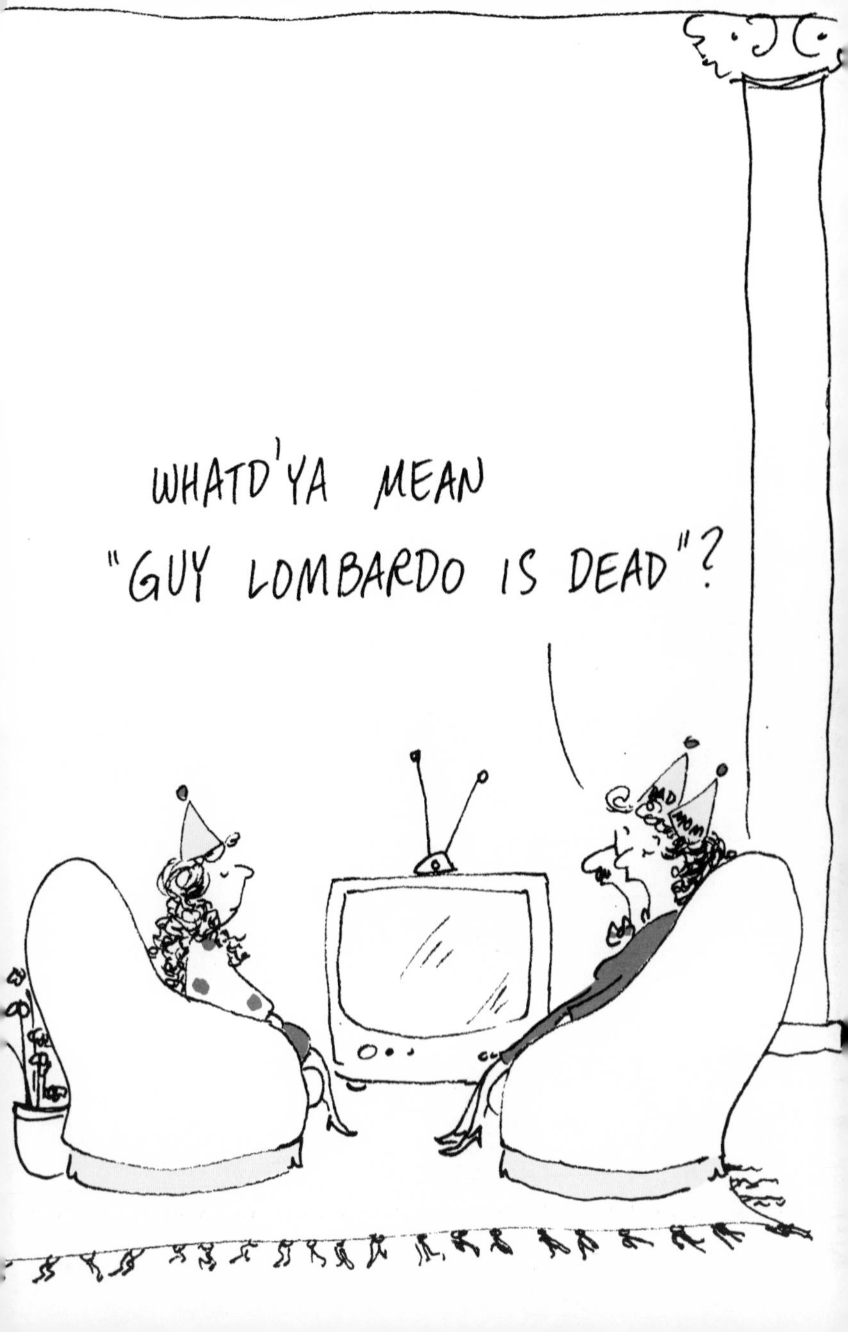
WHATD'YA MEAN
"GUY LOMBARDO IS DEAD"?
DAD
MOM

Falling in Love

YOU SEE, I LIVE ALONE AND I FIND THIS IS THE BEST WAY TO GET RID OF LEFTOVERS.

BUNNY RABBIT!

TUNA FISH!

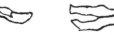

Trouble

ALL I SAID WAS,

" I THOUGHT WE'D CONTINUE DATING LIKE THIS
FOR A FEW YEARS AND THEN MAYBE WE COULD
START SEEING EACH OTHER MORE THAN ONCE
A WEEK. "

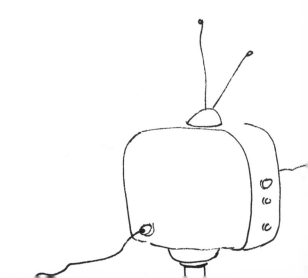

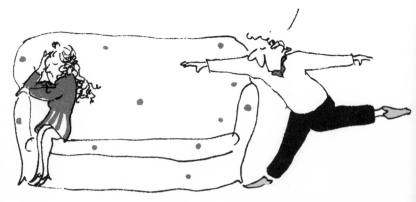

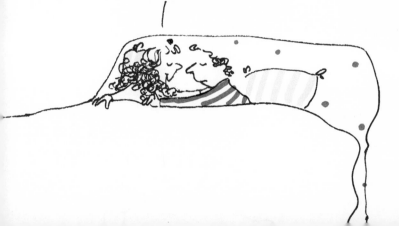

I FIND YOU IN BED WITH MY TWO BEST FRIENDS AND YOU EXPECT ME TO BELIEVE THAT NOTHING IS GOING ON? HAH!
HE'S OBVIOUSLY CHEATING ON ONE OF THEM.

Surviving a Broken Romance

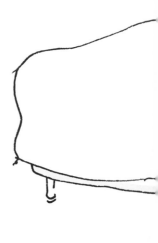

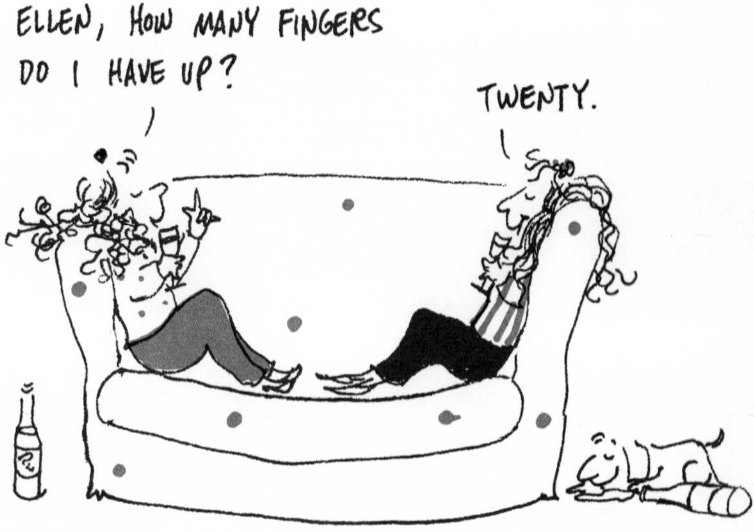
ELLEN, HOW MANY FINGERS DO I HAVE UP?
TWENTY.

Starting Over

I'M GOING OUT FOR A WHILE.
DON'T LET ANYONE IN UNLESS
HE'S TALL, DARK, HANDSOME,
ARTICULATE, AND AVAILABLE.

LARS, I MUST TELL YOU THAT I HAVE
RECENTLY BEEN THROUGH A BROKEN ROMANCE
AND I SIMPLY CAN'T GET INVOLVED WITH ANYONE
RIGHT NOW DUE TO MY FRAGILE AND VULNERABLE
STATE.

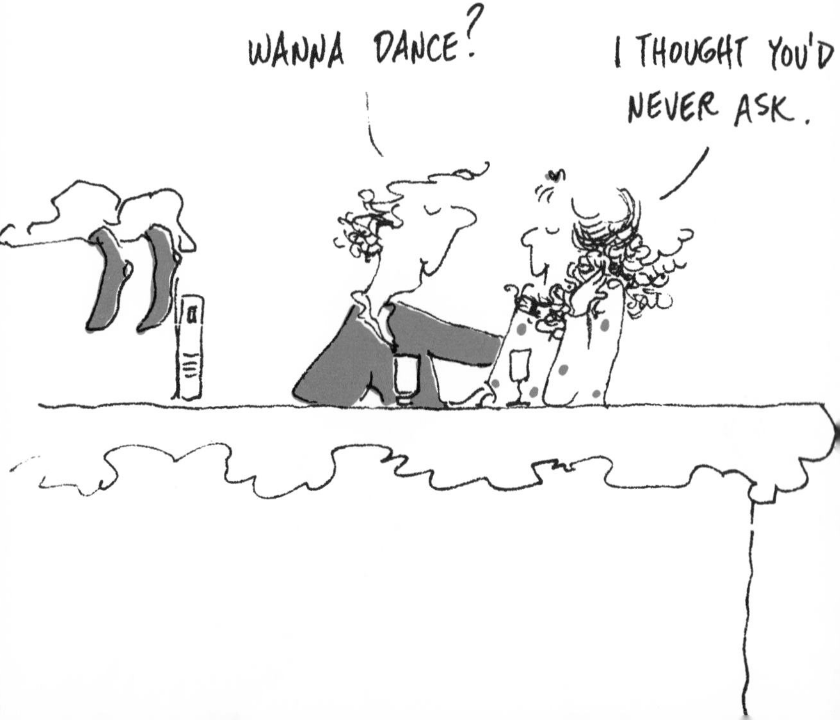
WANNA DANCE?
I THOUGHT YOU'D NEVER ASK.

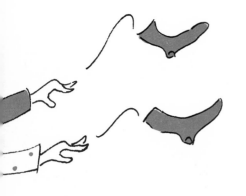